DATE DUE

MCA			

DEMCO 38-296

I Want to Be
AN
ASTRONAUT

By Michaela Muntean
Illustrated by Joe Ewers

A SESAME STREET/GOLDEN PRESS BOOK
Published by Western Publishing Company, Inc.,
in conjunction with Children's Television Workshop.

9.95

CC 34141

My little brother, Elmo, and I watched
a space shuttle take off. We watched it on TV.
It was so exciting!

9.95

CC34141

We listened to the countdown. "3...2...1...blast off!"
There was a loud roar and big clouds of smoke. Then
the rocket zoomed up into the sky.

The astronauts were inside the space shuttle.
Someday I am going to ride inside a rocket ship, too.

I asked my mommy if there is an astronaut school.

She said, "Yes, because there are so many things an astronaut has to learn."

"Like what?" I asked.

"Let's go to the library and find out, Daisy," said my mommy.

The librarian helped me find a book about astronauts. I checked it out and took it home.

My mommy is right. There are so many things astronauts have to know! One of the most important is learning how to do their jobs in a place where there is no gravity.

Gravity is what keeps our feet on the ground. Without it, we would float around in the air. In space that is just what happens, because in space there is no gravity.

My book says that floating in the air feels a lot like floating in water, so astronauts practice in a big swimming pool. I think that sounds like fun.

ALL ABOUT
ASTRONAUT

When astronauts finish their training, they are ready to be part of a crew on a rocket ship. Before they take off, they pack a bag. The astronauts bring socks and underwear and pajamas.

Most of the time they wear flight suits. The suits have lots of zip-up pockets so the astronauts' pens and pencils and notebooks won't float away.

I told Elmo all the things I've learned so far.

"How do they keep their food from flying away?" he asked.

It was a good question, and I found the answer in my library book.

The astronauts' food comes in little containers.
When they are ready to eat, they snap the containers
into trays. Then they fasten the trays to their laps so the
food doesn't float away while the astronauts are eating.

"Wouldn't it be funny to see peas and hot dogs
floating through the air?" Elmo said.

Elmo and I looked at the pictures in my book.

"Where do the astronauts sleep?" he asked. "I don't see any beds."

"Maybe they are too excited to sleep," I said.

But then we read that astronauts have to rest just like everyone else. They take off their flight suits and put on their pajamas. Then they zip themselves into sleeping bags that are attached to the walls of the spaceship. That way they won't drift around and bump into things while they're asleep.

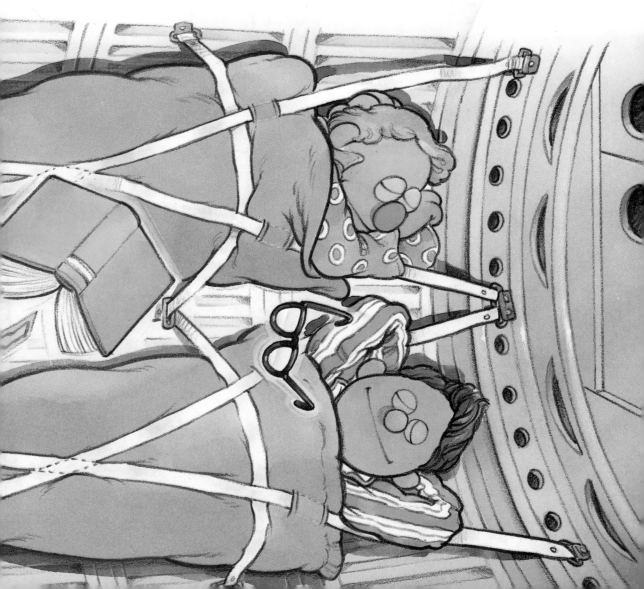

The astronauts live and work in an area at the front of the spaceship. There are lots of windows. They can look out the windows and see Earth as they fly around it.

They can see mountains and deserts. They can see oceans and cities. When I'm an astronaut, I wonder if I'll be able to see my house from the spaceship.

"Will you wave to me when you fly by?" Elmo asked.

I said, "Of course I will!"

Sometimes the astronauts have to go outside the rocket ship to fix something, or to take pictures. In space there is no air to breathe, and it can be very cold or very hot. The astronauts wear big spacesuits to protect themselves. They also wear backpacks with tanks of air for them to breathe.

Astronauts' helmets have earphones and a microphone inside so they can talk to each other.
They also wear little rockets that snap onto the backpacks so they can fly around by themselves. I think that sounds like the most fun of all!

Elmo asked if I would be able to bring one of the little rockets home with me after my trip into space. I told him I didn't think so.

"Too bad," he said. "It would be so much fun to fly around Sesame Street."

I close my eyes for a second and imagine what it would be like to float up in the sky at night.

Someday I will wear a spacesuit and a little rocket on my back. Someday I will zip around in a spaceship taking pictures of Earth, or maybe even Mars.

When I grow up, I want to be an astronaut!